IONA AND THE IONIANS.

THEIR

𝕸anners, 𝕮ustoms, and 𝕿raditions,

WITH

A FEW REMARKS

ON

MULL, STAFFA, AND TYREE.

BY

W. MAXWELL.

MDCCCLVII.

IONA, *July*, 1857.

MY DEAR SIR DUNCAN,

Knowing the deep interest you take
in everything connected with the Highlands of
Scotland, but more particularly your native
County, Argyleshire, allow me to Dedicate the
following pages to you, as a very small token
of my regard, and as a proof that I do not
forget the "days o' lang syne," when I had the
honour and pleasure of serving under your com-
mand, in the 79th Highlanders. Trusting you
may overlook (as of old) my numerous imperfections and deficiencies,

I remain,

Yours very sincerely,

W. MAXWELL.

Sir D. M'DOUGALL.

Contents.

List of Illustrations.

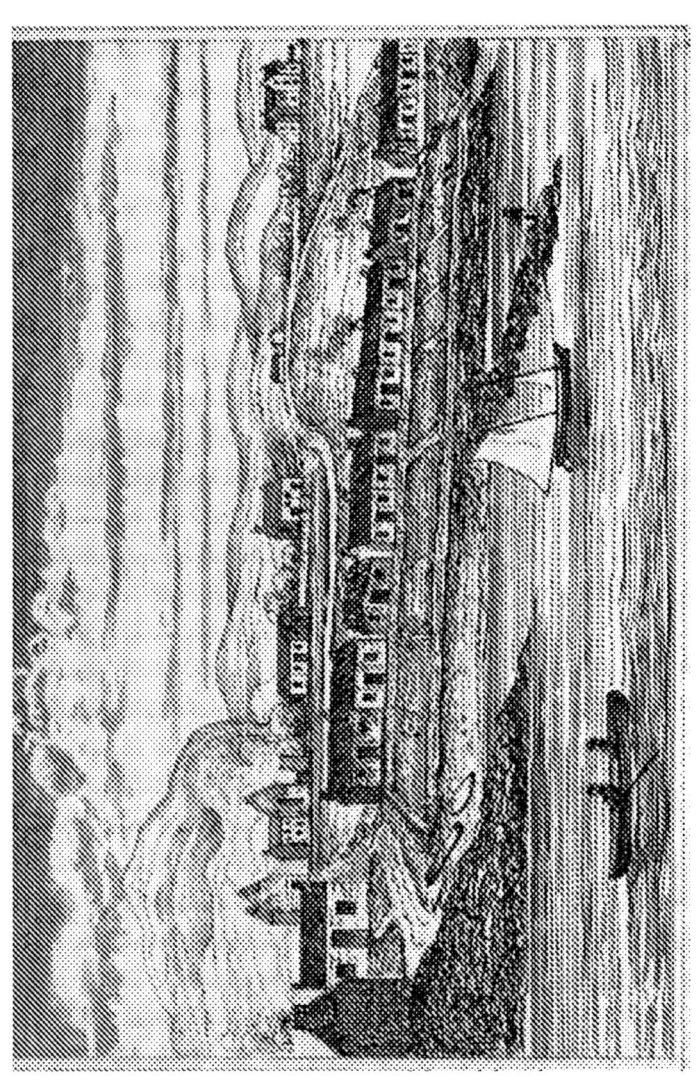

EDITOR'S HOUSE, SHELL CITY, MINN.

1904

IONA AND THE IONIANS.

AUTHENTIC history furnishes no precise data of the first settlement in Iona, but the earliest traditions which can be relied on, inform us that amidst its then woods and groves the ancient and powerful Order of Druids "ruled the land." Traces of them (as will be seen in the sequel) are still numerous throughout the island.

The pervading and all-powerful influence of Christianity, however, under the teaching of Columba and his faithful disciples, invaded idolatry here, as elsewhere, and ere long the cross was planted where the sacred groves had flourished.

The Druids were expelled from Iona, and the light of Christianity first dawned on benighted Scotland.

It is not a little remarkable that no record should

B

have been handed down to us of the date of this most important event. It is lost " in the womb of time." Suffice it, that in Iona a church was planted, which, though small at first, nourished by the living waters of the Gospel, grew and flourished, until its fame was spread throughout the then civilised world.

It is not our present purpose to dwell on the rise and progress of Christianity in our land; *that* we leave to those more competent for the task. *Our* object is to direct the attention of Tourists and strangers who may visit this part of Argyle-shire, to such interesting remains of " the light of other days " as may still exist in Iona and its neighbourhood; also to the manners, customs, and traditions of the inhabitants, etc., etc., trusting that (imperfect though our labours are) such information as the following pages contain may prove of some little interest to the Tourist, and, mayhap, add " here a little, there a little " to his knowledge of the once celebrated Icolmkill.

Facts, historical and local, concerning a place once so celebrated as Iona, may not be altogether devoid of interest, especially since its fame is, in some respects, co-extensive with literature and civilisation.

IONA.

The earliest local traditions relative to this island inform us that, before the Christian era, the powerful and mysterious Order of Druids were the recognised instructors of the people in matters social and religious throughout the entire of Great Britain. But, as the resplendent light of Christianity spread its benign influence and warmth among the nations, the Druids, driven westwards from the richer and more populous districts, did at length find an asylum on the solitary shores of Iona, and there, in its groves, rear their characteristic altars, and kindle their sacred fires. Through the same traditional channel we learn that the oak then flourished here, in all its native magnificence and strength, a circumstance to which we give full credit, as remnants of these mighty "monarchs of the woods" have been occasionally turned up by the inhabitants in the mosses, and it is by no means a rare thing to find large quantities of acorns imbedded deeply in the same. Time, however, changes all things, and at this day the oak as a tree is unknown on the island.

In proof of the druidical "light of other days," and of their numbers in this locality, the stranger has still pointed to his notice "Cladh-nan-Druidhneach," the burying-ground of the Druids, in which, when the peasant is at work, skulls and other relics of mortality are frequently turned up. From the gigantic size of these, the archæologist and phrenologist would doubtless deduce inferences of absorbing interest.

The lessons of the Druids sank deep into the ardent minds of the Celtic race, and to this fact is unquestionably referable the long-continued prevalence of the superstitious ideas and practices which *did* and *do* characterise the inhabitants of the Western Highlands; for, among them, it is still considered a sacred duty to transmit from sire to son the opinions, maxims, ceremonies, and beliefs of their ancestors.

The druidical influence, however, began to de-

cline on the arrival of St Columba and his twelve
disciples, in the year of grace 563. This saint,
unlike many of the moderns, was highly dis-
tinguished for extraordinary piety, talent, and
attainments. Though related to the kings of
Ireland and Scotland, so unambitious was he of
mere worldly renown, that he renounced the ordi-
nary avenues to fame, for the purpose of conse-
crating all his energies to the great task of
enlightening and evangelising the pagan inhabitants of these western regions. In his case we
see the wonderful success and impetus that can
be given by the concentrated powers of one great
character to an enterprise, when such happens to
be worthy of the fostering care of Heaven.

The bay in which Columba and his followers
landed is called "the bay of the wicker boat,"
from the description of vessel in which they crossed
from Ireland. Here is a green mound, tradition-
ally said to give a correct representation of the
boat in which the apostle arrived on his holy
mission. On landing, he took the precaution to
bury his boat in the earth, to prevent return, in

the event of any of his companions being seized with a "home sickness" more potent than their missionary devotion. In the bay already mentioned are seen numerous piles of stones, similar to those "cairns" which are observable in different parts of Scotland. These piles, of all sizes, are said to have been erected as a penance, on the bare and bended knee, by individuals who had rendered themselves obnoxious to the severe Ecclesiastical discipline of the Druids. *If* the heaps *were* proportioned to individual cases of delinquency, then, among them there must have been sinners of the deepest dye.

On the shore of this bay are to be found fine specimens of serpentine and hernblende. To the east of this spot are the marble quarries, which, though not at present worked, yielded in former times a supply of excellent quality, white as well as coloured.

Amongst the cliffs on the south-western part of the island, a singular phenomenon presents itself, designated the "spouting cave." When the wind is high, and the surging billows large, the water,

in a columnar form, rises to the height of about
200 feet, presenting a view equally grand and
romantic. This is to be accounted for by the
compression of the air in the cave, owing to the
strong influx of the waves, and the repercussion
consequent on their reflux produces the said
phenomenon. When the spouting cave is in full
play, it possesses at once both novelty and grandeur.
Adjacent to the spouting cave, on a lofty pinnacle,
appears a "cairn," said to have been erected by
Columba, and denominated by him *"Carn-cul-ri-
Erin,"* a Gaelic phrase expressive of his bidding
farewell to Ireland.

In the immediate vicinity of this spot (port-a-
churich), is *"port Lathrican,"* where we find remains of a former settlement. This must evidently have been the first attempt at colonisation
made by Columba and his followers in Iona.
Amongst other ruins, we clearly trace the foundations of a religious edifice, not only from its
peculiar form, but likewise from the size and
position of the ruins. Around it are vestiges of
numerous circular dwellings. No record which

can be relied on has descended to our time respecting the exact nature of these ruins; but, as noticed above, tradition assigns "port Lathrican" as the first settlement of our "pilgrim fathers" in Caledonia.

On the east side of the island there is a small crescent-shaped, beautiful inlet, called "Martyr's Bay," so styled in consequence of many saints having been there drowned by a roving band of northern barbarians, when on one of their predatory excursions so common in these "good old times."

Immediately above this is the interesting green mound, the "Hill of Mourning," whereon, from time immemorial, all bodies brought to Iona for interment were laid, preparatory to the adjustment of the funeral procession. This custom is still observed. "Relig Oran," or St Oran's burying-ground, is the principal, and now the sole place of interment on the island. In this consecrated spot there lie the remains (so saith tradition) of forty-eight Scottish kings, four of Ireland, eight of Norway, and one or two of France, be-

sides those of abbots, chieftains, and others of
lesser note. Indeed, from discoveries constantly
made, the whole of Iona must have been in times
past reckoned as sacred ground, and made by be-
lievers one vast cemetery, wherein to rest in peace
their weary bodies, when "life's fitful dream was
o'er."

NUNNERY.

The Nunnery of St Augustine, although now
much dilapidated, yields evident traces of what it
must have been in the "palmy" days of Catho-
licism. Here we may appropriately exclaim,
"Ichabod, Ichabod," for, in lieu of the matin
song or the vesper hymn reverberating through
aisle and chancel, we have the whistling of the
starling and the cawing of the jackdaw. Within
the ruined walls may be seen the last resting-
places of some of its former inhabitants. The
tombstone of (the Prioress) Anna, who was Prioress
of Iona in the beginning of the sixteenth century,
possesses the greater interest, as the Latin inscription thereon indicates the rank and virtues

of the illustrious deceased. In a solitary corner,
separated from the rest of her sleeping sisters, lies
all that was earthly of a nun, who had, by listening to certain emotions of the human heart, de-
parted from the strict observance of her vows.—
"*Requiescat in pace.*"

MACLEAN'S CROSS.

Between the Nunnery and the Cathedral stands
"Maclean's Cross," about twenty-one feet high,
beautifully carved, with a representation of the
Crucifixion on one of its sides. This cross is supposed to be one of the most ancient Christian
relics extant in our country, having been erected
as far back as the sixth century.

ST MARTIN'S CROSS.

Nearly opposite the entrance to the Cathedral,
the cross of "St Martin" towers, arresting the
eye by its massive appearance. History informs
us, that at one period there were upwards of three
hundred crosses throughout Iona, but now, with
the exception of the two above noticed, they have

Tombstone of
THE PRIORESS ANNA.

MACLEAN'S CROSS.

scarcely left a trace to mark their once venerated foundations. On the ruin of the monastic orders, these crosses were by ruthless hands destroyed or carried away. There is strong evidence for the belief that the well-known handsome crosses which adorn the towns of Inverary and Campbelltown had their original "locale" in Iona.

MOUNDS.

In sundry places throughout the island, there rise singularly shaped mounds, so regular in their formation, that it requires no great stretch of the imagination to believe that nature must have been aided by the hand of labour. Tradition affirms that these have been frequently favoured by Angelic appearances, and hence their name of "Angel's hills." If Angels do visit this sin-burdened earth from time to time, the sunny spots in question would doubtless form a most appropriate footstool for such celestial visitants.

DUN. I.

"Dun. I.," the highest hill on the island, is

about 350 feet above the level of the sea. Thither St Columba was wont to retire for private meditation. From its summit a commanding view of all the surrounding isles is obtained. On the north—

> " Ulva dark, and Colonsay,
> And all the groups of islets gay
> That guard famed Staffa round."

On the west—

> " Wild Tyree and Sandy Coll."

On the east, the long winding island of Mull and the blue hills of Morven looming in the distance. On the south, Scarba, Jura, Isla, and Colonsay. Close to "Dun. I." in a northerly direction, the antiquarian finds an object of great interest in " Cobha Culdich," or, the *Culdees' Cells*. Tradition informs us that on this spot the Culdees followed their avocations, and performed their religious rites. With the exception, however, of a few round circles and mounds, nothing *now* is visible " to point a moral or adorn a tale."

WIVES' ISLAND.

In the sound which separates Iona from Mull, a

rocky isle, called "Ivillan-nam-Ban," the "Wives' Island," rears its weather-beaten head. To this barren spot legendary lore tells us that the pious Columba, disturbed in his avocations by the contentions of the frail sex, banished them *en masse*, together with the cows, alleging as his reason for so doing, that "where there is a cow, there will be a woman, and that where there is a woman, there must be mischief." Piety the saint must have had, but if this sweeping banishment of the fair sex really took place, gallantry he could have none.

DR. JOHNSON'S TOUR.

We might expatiate much more fully on the bygone glories of Iona, but, in lieu thereof, we content ourselves by inviting all who desire to enjoy a few days profitably, as well as pleasantly, to go and "*tread that illustrious island, which was once the luminary of the Caledonian regions, whence savage clans and roving barbarians received the benefits of knowledge* and the blessings of religion." At the present time (1857), there are not more than two hundred inhabitants, old and young, in Iona, and every year the number is decreasing. Emigration thins their ranks, added to which, situations in the low country daily tempt the youth of both sexes to push their fortunes and better their conditions in life. Notwithstanding the paucity of people, there are two churches on the island, the Established Church of Scotland, and the Free Church, in addition to which, there is a Baptist preacher. Education is cared for; the parochial school being ably conducted and numerously attended, especially during the winter season, when no labour out of doors withdraws the attention of the pupils from their studies. The village, or *par excellence*, "Ballymore," (meaning thereby "the Great Town,") boasts of an inn, such as it is, but being conducted on temperance principles, Donald is not guilty of "taking his ease" therein. Apart from fishing, weaving is the principal occupation of the people, added to that, we must not forget two sons of Crispin, a tailor, and a brace of "general merchants." Neither must we omit the

post-office, the keeper of which, "a ruler in Israel," combines in his own person nearly all the trades in the island, besides being a "man in authority," as cicerone to the ruins during the summer season, the which, unless "common report" greatly err, is worth all the others put together.

AGRICULTURE.

Agriculture in Iona is still at a low ebb; many reasons tend to this, but the chief cause is, the invincible repugnance ever manifested by the Gael to forsake the beaten paths of his forefathers. Added to which, the island being subdivided into small "holdings," or pieces of land attached to the respective cottages, there is no field for an enterprising agriculturist; consequently, *in re* farming here, as it was in the beginning, so is it now, and such, we much fear, it ever will be, so long, at all events, as the present system continues. Throughout the entire island, even in the most secluded and inaccessible spots, we discover numerous traces of former cultivation during the good old times.   Verily, if the monks did nothing else, they knew how to make the most of their land. At present, notwithstanding all former sad experience of disease and failure in the potato crop, the Ionians cling to that (to them) staff of life with the utmost tenacity. It is still the staple crop of the island, although, alas! too frequently of late years "filled with wounds, and bruises, and putrifying sores." Wheat is not grown here; oats are only partially cultivated; the principal grain crop being bear, or barley, and occasionally a field or two of rye. Here and there may be seen a small patch of turnips, which, judging from their luxuriant appearance, thrive well. But the great drawback to all proper agriculture in Iona is the total want of fences; for here there is no subdivision of property, no landmarks to signify to a neighbour that "thus far shall he come, but no farther." Consequently, broils and disputes are too common amongst the people, the *questio vexata* ever being the old story—a case of trespass and damage.

Manure, properly so called, is not applied to the land; in lieu thereof, during the winter months

a top dressing of sea-weeds is spread on the sur-
face, which in spring is ploughed in. There is no
regular succession of crop, so, year after year the
originally poor soil becomes more and more im-
poverished, until at length weeds and thistles
almost carry the day. As to any improvements
in agricultural implements, such are not to be
looked for here. ¯ The old-fashioned, clumsy
wooden plough, with few exceptions, continues in
general use. Owing to the want of water, and
other reasons, thrashing-mills, etc. etc. are not—
the flail doing the work.

The pasture here is of excellent quality, as the
milk and butter testify, but of both articles there
is at all times a very limited supply, and during
the latter end of winter and spring even that fails.
Of late years, as the demand in the low country
for pork increases, the people, when they can
manage it, generally fatten one or more pigs, not,
however, for their own consumpt, pork being in
their eyes unclean! and therefore forbidden, consequently they go to "pay the rent." Until a
change takes place in the present system, little or

no improvement can be looked for; but were the island only divided into two farms, with enterprising tenants, then old things would pass away, and we are confident that Iona would once more be even as a garden, and " blossom as the rose."

INDUSTRY.

Failing fishing, and the necessary agricultural work, weaving in its different branches is the sole permanent occupation of many of the people in this district; and, we feel certain, that were strangers and tourists visiting our island aware of the fact, and of the excellence of the article to be obtained, they would thankfully patronise the "arts and sciences" as cultivated in the Holy Isle, and gladly carry with them on their return to their distant homes a memento of Iona industry and skill, in the form of woollen plaids and shawls, which would not only serve as a protection to them against the storms of winter, but also cheer the hearts and fill the too generally empty purses of the poor but industrious fabricators.

THE KILT.

It is a subject of general remark by strangers, that amongst the many picturesque objects throughout the highlands and islands, the "Garb of old Gaul" no longer holds a place. And not without reason; for one may travel from St Kilda to Dumbarton, and among the natives the kilt will be found "the exception, not the rule." There are many enthusiastic and patriotic individuals who deplore that such should be the case; but we beg leave to differ from them, and while claiming for ourselves an equal degree of patriotism, we hail the disappearance of the "philabeg" as a sign of the times, being a decided mark of civilisation and the march of intellect. Ere steamboats, freighted with tourists, became general throughout the Highlands, and when the inhabitants were necessarily confined to their native glens, it was far otherwise. Then, the Gael had a pride in appearing at kirk or market in the romantic attire of his fathers, but in these days he has discarded such; and, alas! for Caledonia, the "Garb of old Gaul" is now only to be seen on the spindle-

shanks of some "would-be" Sassenach sportsman,
or. on the poor idiot of the remote Highland
clachan.

GAELIC.

We cannot say that we regret that such a revo-
lution should have taken place in the Highland
costume; but as an admirer of Ossian, we do deplore that the change is not confined to dress
alone, for, from the influence of the same causes,
the Gaelic language is becoming more and more
corrupted. In Argyleshire, the native tongue is
no longer heard in its pristine purity, it being
now a mixture of lowland terms and phrases, the
which, were Ossian of poetic memory to re-appear
amongst his countrymen, would cause him to exclaim, Alas! what a change is here!

FERRY.

Notwithstanding these days of progress in which
we live, "old things have not yet passed away;"
in proof of which we have only to notice the barbarous and cruel custom prevalent among the

Ionians, of causing their cattle to "shift for themselves," when transporting them from one neighbouring island to another. The sound between Iona and Mull is upwards of a mile in breadth, and in it a very strong tide constantly runs. The inhabitants of the former, in the absence of any proper-sized or safe ferry-boat, are in the use and wont of swimming their horses and cattle from shore to shore. Mr Martin's Act is assuredly not enforced in these parts, for it is painful to witness the poor animals staggering and "groaning in the flesh," on reaching their desired haven. What a powerful sway does the influence of the past wield over those interested, when they do not perceive the necessity for some change in this respect! Surely the sooner a proper ferry-boat is procured, the sooner will the inhabitants find it beneficial to "their ways and means."

LANDING-PLACE.

The want of a quay, or safe landing-place, at Iona, forms a general complaint. Tourists, on disembarking from the steam vessels, have to

scramble on shore, through rocks and pools, to
the no small uneasiness of body, and discom-
posure of mind. · Sundry misshapen rocks rudely
piled together constitute that which, *pro forma,*
is styled a quay! If the noble proprietor does
nothing to remedy this, we are inclined to think
it is the duty of the owners of the steam packets
which ply on this station to erect a safe and proper landing-place for the convenience of their
passengers. · It would be but a graceful compli-
ment to that island from which they derive so
rich a harvest every season.

ROADS.

When on this subject, we cannot omit noticing
the very deplorable condition of the roads throughout Iona. If there is nothing "rotten in the state
of Denmark," most assuredly there is something
very decidedly so in that of the roads here.
Throughout Iona, of Macadam and his art the
inhabitants are in a state of "blessed" ignorance.
There is not a road, properly so termed, in Iona;
the only thoroughfare leading across the island to

the various farm-houses and cottages almost defies description, as much as it does the unfortunate wayfarer when he attempts to pass along it. In wet weather, particularly, it is as a "slough of despond," being then a quagmire of the most yielding nature, absolutely impassable to either man or beast. As to vehicles, they are out of the question. It is not to be wondered at that the Ionians, who pay their annual assessments towards what is termed road money, should grumble at the manner in which their interests are neglected by " the powers that be."

EMIGRATION.

It is gratifying to think that emigration is not now the frightful bugbear it once was to the hardy inhabitants of the Western Highlands. Every year numerous families leave this district for America, there to secure that comfort and independence which it were vain for them to expect if they remained toiling and moiling in their native country. Within the last few years, upwards of fourscore individuals have emigrated from this district, some to America, but the greater proportion to that "El Dorado" of the present day, Australia. The accounts received from them are in general most encouraging; and, as the best comment on the propriety and advantage of their having left their fatherland, considerable sums of money have, in many instances, been remitted home, to induce their relatives and friends in the old country to follow.

The sturdy patriot may deplore the drainage made on the Celtic race from year to year by such an exodus, when he reflects on the heroic bravery and magnanimous endurance which ever characterised them in the hour of trial and danger, when repelling, at the bayonet's point, the massive phalanx of foreign foes. But, on the other hand, the enlightened philanthropist must rejoice when he considers that his poor countrymen are exchanging a life of constant want and misery in the old world, for one of comparative affluence and ease in the land of their adoption. Such being the case, we would most earnestly urge upon all in similar circumstances, to "go and do so likewise."

SUN-DIALS.

Dividing the hours and regulating time through
the medium of sun-dials has been a practice of
very ancient date among most primitive races.
To a great extent the use of such prevails among
the inhabitants of this district. Though rude in
construction, and devoid of that accuracy which
is supplied by mathematical precision or profes-
sional skill, yet many of them, formed of native
marble slabs, are so adjusted by the self-taught
natural philosophers, as to indicate, weather permitting, true meridian time. Of late years, however, these ancient time-indicators are, like other
good old things, yielding, through the power of
invention—so prominent in these days of resistless
progress—to the more modern clock or convenient
watch, which are now by no means either " few
or far between." During the palmy days of dials,
in the absence of the sun—no unusual event here,
when shrouded in mist, or obscured by clouds—
the want of all punctuality in the routine of life,
and in the attendance at church and school, must
necessarily have been to those interested a sub-

ject of sore complaint. On this score Greenwich
time is still felt to be a desideratum, and we sus-
pect that a right and proper appreciation of
" winged time " will not be reckoned a prominent
trait of character in these parts until the iron
horse of the railway shall have penetrated the
Western Highlands.

SUPERSTITIONS.

Throughout the Highlands generally, there is
still everywhere to be found much of the old leaven
of superstition.   In no part is it more entire than
in Iona. The good St Columba, when he banished
all venomous reptiles from his Holy Isle, might
also, surely, we think, with a little more fervour,
have included under his ban all the tribes of
ghosts, fairies, and other wandering spirits, who,
if we are to believe common report, are still in
the " habit and repute " of rendering night hideous
throughout certain portions of this otherwise holy
isle of Iona.   For ourselves, we have tried to call
spirits from all their reputed haunts, not only
'midst the deserted ruins of cathedral and nunnery,

but likewise at the witching hour of midnight;
we have visited many other haunts deemed by the
vox populi "far frae cannie," but in vain; "spirit
or goblin damned" alike disregarded our summons,
and the "good people," alias the fairies, have ever
been (to us) invisible. Seeing is believing, we
maintain; but, *per contra*, so also do the Ionians,
almost all of whom have stories "by the hundred"
of personal encounters and rencounters with the
supernatural. To such an extent is their dread
carried, that, with few exceptions, neither old nor
young ever dare to pass the precincts of Cathedral
or Nunnery after nightfall alone. These feelings
are fostered and nourished in the minds of the
young by listening to the oft-told tales of horror
which, during the long nights of winter, are nar-
rated to groups of awe-stricken auditors, whose
primitive custom it is to assemble themselves together, and while away the time in (nautically
speaking) "spinning a yarn."

QUERN MILLS.

   It may not, perhaps, be altogether uninteresting

to notice, that in Iona the ancient " Quern Mill" is still in common use amongst the Ionians, for grinding their grain. Whether this practice was taken along with the Celtic race on their original exodus from the plains of Shinar, or whether derived in more recent times from their intercourse with the Norwegians, we shall not venture to assert. The employment of this primitive mill vividly illustrates that passage in Scripture which says, "Two women shall be grinding at the mill; the one shall be taken, the other left." Till very recently it has been known that, during long-continued storms in winter, when access could not be had to mills of modern construction in the neighbourhood, the majority of the population in Iona had to depend for their supply of meal on this tedious and laborious mode of production.

TRADITION.

There is a tradition connected with the nether stone of a quern, which, strange enough, has its local habitation in a part of the wall of the old Cathedral in Iona, that when it would disintegrate

into its original particles, then the consummation
of all things would surely come. How soon that
event may be, it would be no easy matter for the
uninitiated to determine, from any data furnished
by the stone in question, although one-half of it
is yet to be seen by the venturesome or curious.

ABUNDANCE OF FISH.

Want of energy is the Highlander's besetting
sin. The sea here abounds with the finest descriptions of fish; but, alas! enterprising fishermen
are wanting. In proof of this statement, we need
only enumerate, turbot, halibut, skate, sole, plaice,
and flounders; also salmon, cod, ling, gurnet, sea-
trout, seath, and lythe; as also mackerel and
herrings. Along all our sandy coasts and rocky
shores, lobsters, crabs, and all the lesser kinds of
shell-fish are likewise known to abound. Notwithstanding all these "treasures of the deep"
within reach of the too-often almost starving
Highlander, he will not avail himself of them—he
" canna be fashed."

LAZINESS.

It is lamentable to think that, in this respect, the Ionians much prefer to lead a life of penury and want, rather than earn their bread by the sweat of their brow.

CHURCH-YARDS.

Until now we were under the impression that the Scotch, above other nations, attached certain feelings of reverence to those hallowed spots which contain all that was earthly of their fathers. We allude to the church-yards or burying-grounds. But, alas! "a change has come o'er the spirit of my dream;" for, within the ancient burial-ground of St Oran, as also in the sacred precincts of the adjoining time-honoured Cathedral, we find that sheep and cattle are there permitted indiscriminately "to wanton and to riot." In many places where no "sculptured urn" nor "mural slab" denotes the last resting-place, mayhap, of some mighty monarch or valiant warrior of other days, the simple turf which once indicated that "hic jacet" is too frequently undistinguishable. The

same applies in every respect to the interior of
the Cathedral, where we were shocked to see sundry huge specimens of black cattle roaming at
large, and leaving "their marks" à discretion.
As a Scotchman, and an antiquarian, we most
earnestly protest against all such desecration, and
we sincerely trust that ere it is too late the attention of the noble proprietor, the Duke of Argyle,
may be called to the present disgraceful state of
affairs as regards the ruins of Iona, and that, as a
matter of course, a permanent stop shall be put
to all such evil doings. Amen! Amen!

GAELIC PROPHECY.

There is an ancient and curious Gaelic pro-
phecy respecting Iona, which must be comforting
in the extreme to all interested.   In the verna-
cular, it is as follows:—

> "Seachd bliadna rhoimbh'n bhràth,
> Thig muir thair Eirin ri aon tràth
> Is thair ILA ghuirm ghlais,
> Ach snamhaidh I Cholum clàraich."

The English translation or interpretation of
which we take from "Pennant,"

"Seven years before the end of the World
 A deluge shall drown the nations:
 The Sea, at one tide shall cover Ireland,
 And the green-headed Islay, but Columba's Isle
 Shall swim above the flood."

FORTUNE-TELLING.

The spirit of divination also (if we are to credit all we hear), still has its priests, or rather priestesses, in Iona. There are crones who practise on the credulity of the simple-minded, by professing to foretell the future, in the contents of a tea-pot! This method is termed "reading the cups." From what we learn, their plan of operations is as follows:—Having procured a supply of the fragrant herb from the inquirer into the dread future, the same is speedily converted into that beverage which "cheers but not inebriates." In their case, we may say it *inspires*. For no sooner is the last drop finished, when the mystery of mysteries commences. From certain forms and shapes which the tea-leaves assume in the bottom of a cup, said worthies pretend to deduce not only all that *has been*, but likewise everything that *is to be*. In some rare instances, "more by luck than

good guiding," some of their silly prophecies (so-
called) have actually come to pass! Then the
fame of the "wise woman" extends far and near.
Her fortune, at all events, is made, and hence-
forth the worthless crone, in the character of a
"wierd woman," commands the awe, respect, and
fear of all and sundry amongst her poor and
ignorant neighbours.

There are many other equally absurd and superstitious customs prevalent amongst the Ionians.
Their isolated position in the world perhaps tends
to keep such alive; but having now the blessings
of religion, and the benefits of education, to say
nothing of their now frequent and comparatively
very easy intercourse with the more civilised and
enlightened portions of their country, we may
confidently expect that ere long, as the march of
intellect progresses, so will folly and superstition
retrograde, and that all such fancies and ideas as
we have attempted to describe will then be num-
bered amongst the things that were.

D

AGRICULTURAL IMPROVEMENT.

It has been said with much truth and propriety, that he is a public benefactor who causes a blade of grass to grow where never grass grew before. During a recent excursion through the Ross of Mull to the Ferry of Craignure, we felt the truth of this remark, on witnessing the great improvements and excellent farming carried on by Mr Campbell of Ardfinaig (Chamberlain to his Grace), and by Captain Campbell of Possil, at his seat, Achncroish. Under the able direction of both these gentlemen, what was very recently a quagmire, or land in a state of nature, is now under the best cultivation, and yields crops of every description, which require only to be seen to prove what may be done by energy, perseverance, and skill. It were well that all in the Highlands followed such very laudable examples, as they would not only benefit themselves, and their families and dependants, but also improve, fertilise, and beautify their country.

IONIAN CURIOSITY-SELLERS.

Without ocular demonstration, it is impossible
to conceive the impertinence and pertinacity of
the urchins of Iona in their attempts to effect a
sale of their trifling curiosities. If an individual
notice their selections of pebbles or shells, they
all cluster around him, holding up their treasures
to his very nose, with such an outcry of discordant
voices, as would disturb the equanimity of the
most apathetic. On no day do they appear more
ragged or dirty than on " steam-boat days," with
the view, we suppose, of influencing the tender
sensibilities of the charitable. Woe betide that
hapless tourist whom they find alone, for they
surround him, *nolens volens*, until he opens his
purse strings as a quit-offering. With the exception of the parents of those thus engaged, all
living here reprobate their conduct. The clergy-
men and teacher have no influence over them, as,
when the chance of money's in the case, all other
things give place; they absent themselves from
school in spite of all remonstrances. Unlike
bashful Highland children in general, for bare-

facedness and impudence the youngsters of Iona
might stand side by side with Glasgow juvenile
criminals.

SEA-BATHING AND SUMMER QUARTERS.

In these go-a-head days, when people generally
are desirous of getting away from the "ills o' life,"
as well as the toils and cares of business, it is a
matter of surprise to us that the public attention
has not yet been directed to the far-famed Island
of Iona as a place for sea-bathing and healthful
recreation. We are persuaded that, should the
noble proprietor be induced to grant feus on his
property here, the public would hail the same as
a most acceptable boon, the more so, as of late
years the desire has been to remove as far as pos-
sible from the busy haunts of men. On this
account, the sacred shores of Iona are second to
none in the world for such a realisation. Already (during the season) steamboats ply three
times per week from Glasgow to Iona, and we
are confident that strangers would gladly sojourn
here for a few days, provided a good hotel and

suitable lodgings were to be procured. To our own knowledge such are often in request, but as these *desiderata* cannot be supplied, the admirers of this locality, however reluctantly, have to retrace their steps. We lament that this should be, for we are convinced that were it otherwise, the now comparatively deserted shores of Iona would assume a very different aspect. Independent of its world-renowned Cathedral and cloisters, the natural curiosities to be seen on the island are neither few nor far between. Should fishing be deemed indispensable, the Sound of Iona abounds with finny tribes of the choicest descriptions, and the neighbouring island of Mull presents fresh water angling in perfection. The climate of Iona is salubrious in the extreme, in proof of which we have only to call attention to the numerous very old inhabitants who enjoy a green old age.

PEATS.

In Iona there is little or no turf, *Scottice*, peat, consequently all the fuel burned by the inhabitants has to be cut and prepared in the mosses of

Mull. For this reason, during the storms of winter, the Ionians are frequently almost destitute of firing for weeks together. When we think of the trouble they are put to, ere they can even boil a kettle, their fuel is indeed dearly purchased; nay, may we not also add, dangerously, considering that crossing the Sound of Iona in a frail and overloaded open boat is not always unattended with risk?

GAME.

The sportsman has not a large field for his operations here. During the spring there are a few woodcocks, and a tolerable number of snipe; for a couple of months in midsummer, landrails are very numerous. Wild-ducks abound during the season; amongst others the eider, so celebrated for its down. It is not generally known that the stormy petrel, *vulgo*, "Mother Carey's chicken," breeds on one or two of the neighbouring rocky isles. There are a few rabbits on the island, but as there must be a scarcity of food for them during winter, their numbers never increase.

Hawks and other birds of prey abound. The Norwegian rat, as in other places, is here at home. The following is a list of the rare descriptions of birds found on or near Iona; it was prepared by an English gentleman, Mr Graham, lately resident on the island.

WILD FOWL—NATATORES.

Wild Swan, or Hooper—Cignus Ferus.
Barnacle Goose—Anser Leucopsis.
Common Sheldrake—Tadorna Belonii.
Widgeon—Mareca Penelope.
Goosander—Mergus Mergansor.
Great Northern Diver—Colymbus Glacialis.
Green Crested Cormorant—Phalacrocorax Christatus.
Solan Goose—Sula Bassana.
Arctic Tern—Sterna Artica.
Red-breasted Merganses—Mergus Serrator.
Stormy Petrel—Thalassidroma Pelagica.
Eider Duck—Somateria Molissima.
Long-tailed Duck—Harelda Glacialis.
Red-headed Pochard—Fuligula Ferina.

GRELLATORES, ETC.

Heron—Ardeci Cinerea.
Woodcock—Scolopax Rusticula.
Common Snipe—Scolupax Gallinago.
Jack Snipe—Scolupax Gallinula.
Godwit —Limosa Rufa.
Turnstone—Strepsilas Interpres.
Curlew—Numenius Arquata.
Whimbrel—Numenius Pheopus.
Lapwing—Vanellus Christatus.
Grey Plover—Squaterola Cinerea.
Golden Plover—Squaterola Pluvialis.

RAPTORES.

Merlin—Falco Œsalon.
Kestrel—Falco Tennunculus.
Hen-harrier, or Ringtail—Circus Cyaneus.

The great Golden Eagle is occasionally seen here.

OONIROSTRES.

Raven—Corvus Corax.
Hooded Crow—Corvus Cornix.
Red-legged Crow—Fregilus Graculus.
Jackdaw—Corvus Monedula.
Starling—Sturnus Vulgaris.
Carrion Crow—Corvus Corone.

SONG BIRDS.

Thrush—Mercula Musica.
Blackbird—Merula Vulgaris.
Red Wing—Merulis Iliaca.
Linnet—Linaria Canabina.
Skylark—Alauda Arvensis.
Yellow-hammer—Emberiza Cetrinela.
Snow-bunting—Plectrophanes Nivalis.
Rock Pipit—Anthus Aquaticus.
Wheatear—Saxicola Œnanthe.
Redbreast—Saxicola Rubicola.

RASERES.

Blue Rock Dove—Columba Livia.
Black Grouse—Tetras Tetrix.

Besides birds, there are the

Seal—Phoca Vitulina.
Otter—Mustilla Lutra.
Rabbit—Lepus Cuniculus.

Weasel—Mustilla Vulgaris.
Field Mouse—Mus. Sylvaticus.
Common Mouse—Mus. Musculus.
Rat—Mus. Decumanus.

GEOLOGY.

The rocks on the north-eastern side of the island are composed of quartz, combined with chlorite and hornblende. They are, however, subject to much variety, passing on the one hand to hornblende rock and clay slate, and on the other into a siliceous calcareous slate. These rocks are traversed throughout by veins of the "granites garbengensis" of Linnæus. The same strata continues to the north-east extremity of the island, where they give place to hornblende slate, sienite, and hornblende rock, bearing much the appearance of serpentine. These rocks alternate, and are to be observed crossed by basalt and granite veins. Towards the hill of Dun I., the hornblende and sienite strata form on some parts of the coast cliffs of considerable height. This hill is composed of primitive rock and hornblende slate. On the south-west shore are very extensive rocks of sienite, vivid in colour, extremely

hard, and susceptible of a high polish. Of this
substance, most of the remains of antiquity here
are composed. Immense veins of beautiful serpentine stretch along the southern extremity, of
a pleasing green shade, often clouded with other
colours. At Port-a-churich, the cliffs are likewise formed of hornblende, having much the
appearance of serpentine and sienite. In this
direction we also discover jasper of very fine
quality; and here are found nodules of nephriticus,
varying in size from a pea to that of an apple,
these are green and transparent, and are made
into trinkets. They are (or were) also worn as
amulets or charms of anti-magical and medicinal
virtue.

The shore is here rugged and bare, and near it
are several small islands and rocks entirely composed of red granite. Geologists conjecture that
at an early period in the history of our planet,
this island was probably joined to the granite
coast of Mull, and separated therefrom by some
convulsion of nature. Appearances are most un-
doubtedly in favour of such a theory. A stratum

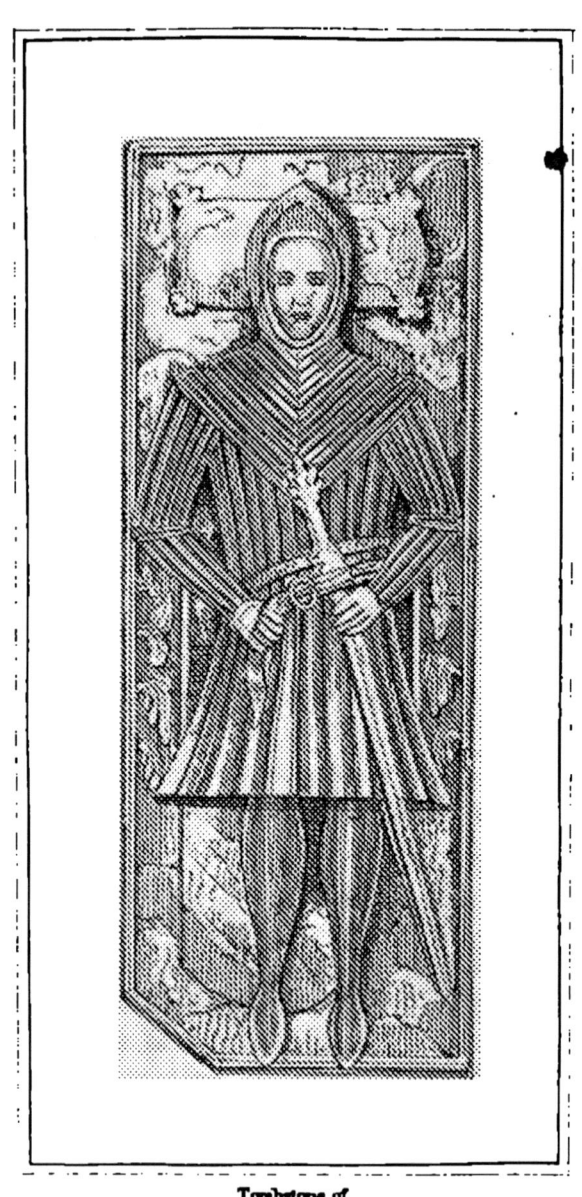

Tombstone of
MACLEAN OF LOCHBUY

of white and coloured marble, from thirty to forty
feet thick, running or lying north-north-west, is
on the south-east coast of the island. It has been
worked, but, as stated elsewhere, its value did
not cover the expense attending the labour.

ST ORAN'S CHAPEL.

The remains of this edifice are now in a state
of picturesque ruin, there being few traces of its
former beauty left " to point a moral or adorn a
tale." The building is supposed to be of much
older date than the present Cathedral—the sixth
century being assigned as the probable period of
its erection. It presents a small rude structure,
built of red granite, but, as elsewhere, the destroying hand of time has done its work here. The
entrance doorway is nearly entire, and forms a
fine specimen of the then architecture; but the
principal object of interest is the very elegant
" Triple Arch," supposed to have been originally
over the high altar, or (in our humble opinion)
more probably to have formed the ornamental
part of some tomb, now unknown. There are

several elegantly carved and inscribed stones
within its walls, amongst which, from the cogni-
zance, are to be noticed those sacred to the
memory of the Lords of the Isles.

> " Lords of the Isles, whose mighty name
> A thousand bards have given to fame."

The powerful and ancient Clan of M'Quarrie are
here also represented in the sculptured effigies of
three grim warriors, armed "to the teeth." The
M'Donalds of Kintyre, "heirs of mighty Somer-
led," warriors all "stout and strong," here also
rest in peace. Macleans of various septs, Duart,
Lochbuy, Coll, Grulin, etc., etc., who, ere "life's
fitful dream was o'er," were ever waging war one
against the other, now sleep tranquilly within the
burying-ground of St Oran.

Sundry bishops and priors are here interred,
the figures on the tombstones denoting their respective ranks, the mitre, stole, and pastoral staff,
etc. That commonly known as "the four priors
of Iona" deserves notice, were it only for the
inscription, which is in fine preservation, cut in
the old English character:—

𝕳𝖎𝖈 jacent quatuor 𝖕𝖗𝖎𝖔𝖗𝖊𝖘 𝖉𝖊 𝖄, 𝖊𝖙 𝖚𝖓𝖆 nationt: b.
𝕵𝖔𝖍𝖆𝖓𝖓𝖊𝖘, 𝕺𝖚𝖌𝖔𝖓𝖎𝖚𝖘, 𝕻𝖆𝖙𝖗𝖎𝖈𝖎𝖚𝖘, in 𝖉𝖊𝖈𝖗𝖊𝖙𝖎𝖘, olim 𝕭𝖆𝖈𝖚𝖑𝖆-
𝖗𝖎𝖚𝖘, staltur 𝕰𝖚𝖌𝖔𝖓𝖎𝖚𝖘 qui obit anno 𝖉𝖔𝖒𝖎𝖓𝖎 𝖒𝖎𝖑𝖑𝖊𝖘𝖎𝖒𝖔 quin
𝖌𝖊𝖓𝖙𝖊𝖘𝖎𝖒𝖔.

" Here lie four Priors of Y (Iona), all of one clan, John,
Eugene, Patrick, formerly Bachelor in degrees, and a second
Eugene, who died in the year of our Lord 1500."

Our limits do not permit us to enter into all
the details of this most interesting spot, but to
those who thirst after " meditations amongst the
tombs," then we have only to say, pay a visit to
the shrine of St Oran.

CATHEDRAL.

The Cathedral (or rather, the ruins of the same,)
forms the great object of attraction in Iona.
When we consider the probable time of its original erection as a religious establishment, and
more particularly its site, in an island so remote,
secluded, and (may we not add) barbarous, as
Iona must have been, our astonishment is indeed
great. As this ruin has frequently, ere now, been
the subject of remark and illustration, alike by
the poet, historian, and artist, we do not consider
it necessary to dwell at any length in a descrip-

TOMBSTONE of a BISHOP of IONA.

SAINT MARTIN'S CROSS.

BROKEN CROSS, CATHEDRAL.

the original vessel in which the pilgrims of old washed their feet ere entering the sacred fane.

Passing through the arched doorway, the view extends to the great window at the extreme end of the building. Formerly the *coup d'œil* must have been very grand, even now it is so. Here the eye is distracted by the multiplicity of objects claiming attention, and the beautiful but frequently grotesque figures and subjects everywhere exhibited on pillar and column, in high and bas-relief. No two of these are the same. They are chiefly from scriptural subjects, although we are irreverent enough to think that not a few of them are apocryphal. In the area of the building are a few fine tombstones. On one side, apart from, though connected with the body of the building, is what is termed the Chapter House, a groined and vaulted chamber, lighted by a Gothic window; on each side there are vacant niches, evidently intended for statues or images, long since gone hence. Beyond this are the ruins of the so-called library and refectory, as also, the very fine remains of the ancient cloisters. The great tower is lighted by four marigold windows, or Catherine wheels, with spiral windows, the rooks and jackdaws its sole tenants. Not far from this, in the adjoining field, we see the ruins of Dun-i-Manich, or the Monk's Fort, built of stone and lime, and on the other side of the Cathedral, in a similar position, are the remains of a small chapel, which formerly must have been connected with the great building. Tradition only, not history, gives any account of these, and that is so meagre and contradictory, that we shall not enter into the subject, on the principle of the old adage, that "least said is soonest mended."

BLACK STONES OF IONA.

Not many years ago, the antiquities of Iona suffered a grievous loss in the destruction, by a maniac, of the celebrated and curious "Black Stones," which were ever held in great awe from the remotest times. These stones, composed of a single block of dark-coloured granite, curiously carved, were five feet in height and two broad, stood near the entrance to the Cathedral, near the

cloisters. From time immemorial they were held in peculiar veneration. All charters, covenants, and engagements were solemnly attested on them.

Before quitting the Cathedral, we must not forget to state that within its precincts, we are told, the remains of the good St Columba, along with those of his pious attendant, "Dermot," were interred. But all traces of such are gone. The casket is *there*, but the treasure is not. They must have been removed at some early period elsewhere.

The ruins of the Convent, or Nunnery, must not be passed over. There is no record of their first erection. From what remains, however, the Nunnery must have been of large extent. Like the Cathedral and the other ruins, it belongs to no distinct form of architecture—the Gothic being perhaps the more prevalent. The pointed arch and groined roof of the entrance doorway is an object of much interest. Here there are numerous tombstones, many of them of great beauty, as well of form as workmanship. That of a former prioress (as elsewhere noticed), is parti-

E

cularly worthy of remark. Of course they are all
of the holy Sisterhood.

The old proverb hath it, that it is "better late
than never." We rejoice therefore to learn that
the noble proprietor is, at the eleventh hour,
taking steps to preserve what still remains to us
of these celebrated ruins; but at the same time,
we deeply regret to observe that, with a lamentable want of taste, and a total disregard to all
appearances, the magnificent windows in the
Cathedral are, by his orders, actually *all built
up*. To us the appearance of the Cathedral is
now most materially injured; but *Chaq un à
son gout.*

BAGPIPES.

Amongst other distinguishing traits and customs
of the Highlanders, the use of the Great Highland Bagpipe may be said *now* to be remembered
amongst the things that were. With "the philabeg and tartan plaid," the pipes have yielded to
the march of progress. The day is not far distant
when we remember every glen and every hamlet

boasted of its piper; and not a "wedding" or
other merry-making ever took place, but the
welkin rang to the strains of the pibroch.

We know not to what cause such a change is
to be attributed. It is *not* from any want of love
for the music, as it is well known that, be it far
as "pole from pole," and let the Gael only hear
the wild notes of his "ain countrie," and his soul
melts within him. Its strains ever conjure up to
"memory dear" the days, scenes, and friends of
"auld lang syne." At present, however, were it
not for the pipers belonging to our gallant Highland regiments, we much fear that this truly
national instrument would soon only live in the
memory of "the oldest inhabitant."

FEUS.

The island has a tri-weekly post with the main-
land. There is a good school and a tolerable
library. With all these resources we do think
that a fine field is open to the noble proprietor,
not only to benefit himself, adding to his income
by granting feus in Iona, but also promoting the

interests of his fellow-countrymen seeking health
and recreation.

POT I.

Within a mile of the Ferry-house, in the Sound
opposite to Iona, when journeying to the village
of Bunessan, the traveller pauses *en route* to
survey the romantic Loch of "Pot. I." Apart
from its natural beauty, it is of interest as
having been, in the days o' auld lang syne,
the special fish-pond of the abbots of Iona.
Pot I., signifying the Pot of Iona. It is a
lovely sheet of water, the heath-clad mountains
closely embracing it. In the centre is a rocky
islet, where are to be discovered the ruins of an
ancient fortress, but the destroying hand of Time
has done its work too fully to admit of any
certainty as to its former capabilities. Its very
name, if we mistake not, is lost in its antiquity.
Suffice it, that at present it forms a most picturesque object—one that cannot fail to charm and
arrest the pencil and pen of either artist or poet.
Of a truth these Monks of old, in Pot I., had an

eye both to the useful and the ornamental. From
its waters the delicious salmon and the more
delicate trout must have been ofttimes taken to
supply the simple fare, during fasts and Lent, of
the pious brethren of Iona. From personal experience we can attest that their quality is excellent, and their name "is legion." On its sur-
face at all times are to be seen abundance of the
more common descriptions of wild-fowl, but during severe weather, swans, wild-geese, and other
rare feathered strangers, are also very frequently
to be met with.

Pot I. is about three miles (including the
ferry) from Iona, and five from the village of
Bunessan, in Mull, where, should any disciple of
good old Isaak Walton think of taking a "cast"
on our Highland lake, he can thereafter take his
ease in his inn, under the roof-tree of the hos-
pitable Boniface of the Argyle Arms, Bunessan.

VILLAGE OF BUNESSAN.

Bunessan, the market town of Iona, in the
Ross of Mull, is beautifully situated at the head

of Loch Laigh, on the river Nessan, as it joins the sea, hence its name Bunessan, signifying in Gaelic the mouth of the Nessan. At high water this is really a romantic-looking place, the sea in front almost washing the houses, and the lofty mountains of Mull forming a magnificent background; whilst Staffa and numerous other islands appear in the distance. The inhabitants are not numerous. There is a parish church, a good inn, and several excellent shops. The sea affords employment to the people, fish of various descriptions being abundant. During the season Loch Laigh is celebrated for its herrings. In the river Nessan there is good trout-fishing, and in Loch Asapol, about three miles inland from the village, there are also trout of excellent quality, and as numerous as they are good.

To the geologist, the neighbourhood of Bunessan is not without interest. At Ardtun, a few miles distant, are its famous fossil beds, and at Carsaig there are likewise vast beds of fossils, etc., etc. A granite quarry is also worked.

TOBERMORY.

We must not omit some notice of the picturesquely-situated capital of Mull, Tobermory. Romantic is the term we would apply to the appearance of this town—the houses rising in a succession of terraces from the margin of the sea. Its bay may be said to be unequalled in Scotland, and by many it has even been compared to the world-renowned Bay of Naples. On its land-locked bosom the tempest-tossed outward-bound ship finds a haven where defiance can be put to "a' the airts the wind can blow."

MARY'S WELL.

Tobermory, like other towns, boasts of its wonders, one of which only we shall notice—that of Mary's Well, in Gaelic *Tobar Mhoire*, whence it derives its name. On an eminence above the town, in a partial enclosure, the thirsty traveller rejoices at the sight of this gushing fountain, and hastens to cool his parched lips at its limpid stream. Its waters are regarded as possessing qualities and virtues of a highly salubrious and

slightly mineral nature, and on that account they
are much resorted to, not only by the inhabitants
but also by strangers visiting the locality. We
have tested these waters, and can safely affirm
that their qualities have not been exaggerated for
purity, icey coolness, and invigorating tendencies.
Scientific men prove that Mary's Well surpasses
all other springs in this country in these whole-
some properties, which are ever sought for in the
pure element. Tourists should not fail (*en passant*) to pay a hurried visit to this celebrated
well. We feel very confident they will have no
reason to regret their time and trouble.

ST MARY'S LOCH.

Within the ornamental woods surrounding the
mansion-house of Drumfin, in the immediate
vicinity of Tobermory, is St Mary's Loch, which
is well worthy of a visit; as, independent of its
natural beauties all around, it is also well stocked
with those "yellow beauties" which rejoice the
heart of the angler. It abounds with very fine

trout, some of which are of a large size, and all of them most exquisite in flavour.

There is constant communication per steam between the Lowlands and Tobermory, where the stranger is always certain of obtaining "good accommodation for man and beast."

ISLAND OF TYREE.

It is well known that the island of wild Tyree was, during the days of monastic rule in Iona, an appanage to the religious order founded by Columba in that island. The etymology of the word corroborates this statement—*Tir-I*, signifying in Gaelic, the land or granary of Iona. It is situated about eighteen miles in a north-west direction from Iona. From time immemorial it has been celebrated for its productiveness, and to this day it still retains the same prolific character. Oats, barley, and potatoes are its staple products —the latter having had the enviable quality of generally remaining sound, whilst those on the neighbouring islands were being destroyed by the now too prevalent and much-dreaded blight·

Tyree also is renowned for its breed of horses,
conjectured to have originated from the introduc-
tion of some Spanish barbs, which were rescued
from the wreck of one or more vessels composing
part of the great Spanish Armada, known to have
been lost among the Western Isles on their disas-
trous defeat by man and the elements.

Throughout the island there are numerous remains of religious establishments and extensive
cemeteries, the latter vying even with Iona in
their interesting tombstones.

Like Iona, Tyree also must at one time have
been regarded as sacred ground, under the conse-
crating shadow and fostering care of the pious
Columba, its soil being in many places a veritable
Golgotha. The stranger and tourist, when journeying along its shores, or through its arid plains
in the interior, are ofttimes struck by the sad
emblems of mortality which, uncovered from their
sandy beds by the drifting tempest, now bleach
under the storms of the Atlantic.

Until recently, Tyree had an unenviable cele-
brity on account of the numerous and fatal ship-

STAFFA.

wrecks which from time to time occurred on its
rock-bound shores.

SKERRYMORE LIGHTHOUSE.

Such, however, we rejoice to say, is now no
longer the case, for that which of all other objects
cheers most the hardy mariner, and guides him
on his lonely way, is now supplied by the erection
of Skerrymore Lighthouse. We can assure
strangers that a visit to this establishment will
amply repay them for turning their steps a few
miles out of the beaten track of tourists in general.
The intelligent and obliging superintendent of the
lighthouse will, we need scarcely say, be always
too happy to show his "wonder of the deep" to
all such as are desirous of inspecting the highly-
interesting Lighthouse of Skerrymore.

STAFFA.

This unequalled isle is situated about six miles
north from Iona. Much has been written, and
more said of its wonders, but to realise any idea
of them, they must be seen. Its ancient name

was the "Island of Columns," and well does it merit such a designation. Its highest elevation is about one hundred and fifty feet; the sides are generally columnar, resembling in some degree those of the Giant's Causeway. There are numerous caves along its shores, those styled "Mackinnon's," "the Clam Shell," and "Fingal's," being the grandest, are those which chiefly attract the notice of tourists. Towards the north-west end of the island are five small caverns, which, though possessing little beauty, are nevertheless worthy of notice. During calm weather, when there is a swell on the ocean, owing to the rushing of the tide through their apertures, a report is made often equal to that caused by the discharge of heavy ordnance. From this circumstance it has been termed "the great gun of Staffa." The island is uninhabited, save by a few black cattle and sheep, which apparently thrive on the herbage growing on its summit. Here the naturalist may pass a few hours profitably, there being myriads of sea-fowl, many of which are rare. The steam-vessels plying to Iona during summer, always touch at Staffa, weather permitting, to allow their passengers an opportunity of seeing its wonders.

———

Ere concluding these imperfect sketches of Iona and its neighbourhood, we humbly beg to " throw ourselves on the mercy of the court," begging the favourable sentence of our readers. We are too well aware of the numerous imperfections of the preceding pages; but we have done our all—we can no more, especially so far as " the truth, the whole truth, and nothing but the truth," of the various statements is concerned, the which, we beg leave to state, *en passant*, is not the case in a .small work on Iona, issued a few years since, and purporting to have been from the pen of an American clergyman! where, whether owing to gross ignorance or wilful perversity, he most foully libels the Ionians.

To Mr John Barnett, Iona, we return our special thanks for all the information and assistance we have received from him. We also beg to state our acknowledgments to C. A. M'Vean, Esq. of the same island, for the Sketches and Drawings accompanying the Work, after which, our task being finished, we remain,

THE AUTHOR.

Lightning Source UK Ltd.
Milton Keynes UK
UKOW051947240113

205347UK00001B/122/P

9 781446 092637